Copyright

richard@spreadsheetsolutions.biz

www.spreadsheetsolutions.biz

Cover by Richard Sumner

ISBN: 9798559349817

Imprint: Independently published

About the Author

Richard started a business when knowing absolutely nothing about starting a business. He is a spreadsheet specialist, so started Spreadsheet Solutions, a business to make custom spreadsheets for all applications and businesses. He had many years of experience in all sorts of industries before starting his business, so he has a wide range of skills and expertise. Richard learned many lessons during the first 8 years of running a business, some of them the hard way, so he wrote this book to help others avoid the same mistakes.

Richard is married to Wendy, and they both run and work for Spreadsheet Solutions together. They have a son, which is one of their reasons for starting their own business. They both grew up in South Africa, but now live in Kent in the UK.

Table of Contents

Introduction

You may be wondering who I am, why I wrote a book, and why I'm qualified to help you start and run a business. My name is Richard Sumner and I started a business called Spreadsheet Solutions, where I make custom spreadsheets for businesses of all shapes and sizes. Not just financial spreadsheets, but solutions to tackle all aspects of business. This not only gives me a broad overview of business in general, but a good overview of many types of businesses. This is not why I wrote this book, though. The reason for the book is because I struggled with so many things when I started my business. There are resources available, which go into detail about all aspects of business, but I found very few that would tackle a wide range of business concerns and give an overview on each. That is what this book is about. I want to give you an overview on many business concerns, so that you are aware of them and have a starting point if you wish to find out more about any aspect. This book won't solve all of your problems, but hopefully it will give you an insight into all areas of your business and point you in the right direction, to ask the right questions, so that you can answer all of your business questions. I spent years getting stuff wrong, so it took me longer than needed to grow my business. I don't want you to make the same mistakes, so I've put down all of these suggestions in a book. Each chapter deals with a different business aspect. So read through, skip what you don't need, and come back to the parts that you do need as you need them.

Accounting

I'm not going to write too much about accounting, as it would be best to talk to an accountant, but please talk to an accountant. This should be one of the first things that you do, even before you form the business. They can advise if it's best to go as a sole trader or to register a business (see the relevant chapter). This may not only be based on what you want to do, but also where you want to take the business in the future. Sometimes these changes are harder to make later, so it's best to get clear instructions at the start. As I went with a limited company, the first expense I had (before I even paid my own salary) was an accountant. Even if they just do your end of year accounts. Unless you know how to do them, stay away from them. One thing I will say, though: don't be reliant on your accountant to know how your business is doing. If you must wait for the year end accounts before you know how much money you've made, you're in trouble. You need to know what is happening and where you stand each day. Have your own checks and balances. Yes, chat to your accountant so that you aren't entering data twice, and make sure that what you do is useful to them. You are in control, you are responsible, you need to know how the business is running. When I get my end of year accounts, there are no surprises. I know how I have done, well before submitting the books to my accountant. The only thing I am surprised about is that I owe less tax than I thought, because I deliberately over-estimate to cover myself.

One way that accountants are extremely helpful, is to save you money. They should be telling you how best to save money on taxes. I'm not talking about tax dodging, but the right way to do something. For example, is it better to take a higher salary or a lower salary plus dividends? The answer here will differ as the laws change, and as your business grows, so it's best to keep up to date with things like this. A good accountant should keep on top of this and keep you informed. One last thing I'll say is that you should find an accountant who understands you and shares your ambitions. You may end up working closely with your accountant. Even if you don't, they need to advise you on what's best for you. If they share your ethics and ambitions, this becomes a more natural process.

Take home points:

1. Chat to an accountant before even starting the business
2. Work together with them on your record keeping
3. Make sure they keep you informed of law changes
4. Take responsibility for your business finances
5. Work with an accountant who shares your ambitions and ethics

Advertising

This was one of my biggest learning curves when I started my business. I was signing up to every free listing, creating accounts in all social media platforms, and going to every networking event within a wide range of my home. It can be all-consuming if you let it. I will discuss creating a brand as well as marketing in other chapters, so let's look specifically at advertising your products or services. Do you need to do this straight away? Here are some things to consider. What is it that you are selling and who is your target market? The first thing you need to do is answer those two questions. That will set you up for advertising, marketing, and making your brand known. The reason why you ask what you are selling is to determine what the best course of action is. For example, I sell custom-made spreadsheets. I need to explain what that is, why it will help you, and why you need it. If I simply put up a picture of a spreadsheet and a price, it won't help at all. If someone is selling jackets, putting up a picture of a model in a jacket, a price, and a link to your store, may well help. Asking who will buy your product, tells you where you should be advertising. I sell business products, so I'm not marketing or advertising to teenagers. If you sell baby products, you want to hit the new and expecting parents. If you sell something relevant to men or women, you may only need to advertise to either, but not both. Understand what you are selling and why someone would want to buy that, then understand who is most likely to buy it, and have a person (an avatar) in mind. Your ideal client. Then ask, where would they (my ideal client) hang out, and why would they want to buy what I have. Let's look at an example. Let's say that you sold reasonably priced baby clothes. It's no use for you to list on business listing sites or going to face to face networking (at least not to sell). You would check if there are any baby markets happening, and possibly advertise in their brochure. You'd join mother and baby groups on social media. You may see if there are any lists for baby-related products. Your advertising will revolve around getting your products in front of expecting parents, parents, and possibly even grandparents. Yes, many people have babies, so your target market could be anywhere, but don't worry about that. Think of a few places where your ideal client will be, and then target those places. All of this advertising takes time and or money. You don't want to waste either, but you want to get the best return. Think about who you're targeting, why they'd want to buy your product or service, and how to reach them. Make an advert based on why your client wants to buy your product (see marketing for more about this) and then advertise where you think they're most likely to see it. Track the adverts. If the adverts are online, make a special link or use a query string to show you where the traffic to your website has come from. Why? So that you know what's working. If you're advertising in a brochure, give a discount code specific to that brochure so that you can see who uses it. One thing I learned is that business can come from anywhere and everywhere. Knowing where it actually comes from is key to future planning. I have built many spreadsheets to track return on investment (ROI) with regards to advertising. Don't rely on slick salesmen to tell you how much you will make; know your own numbers. If a campaign or advertising venture works and generates a good ROI, do it again. If it fails, ask why so that you can learn from it, and then don't repeat it. Asking why when you fail or succeed is key, so that you constantly can adapt and evolve your advertising to get the best ROI. Don't be afraid to try new things. Some of my best advertising campaigns happened after I said this simple phrase: I wonder if this will work, because I've never seen it done before. Yes, you can learn from the leaders in your industry, but sometimes something unique will perform best. People don't always respond to the same old, same old. Sometimes something new and interesting gets their attention. My last point on advertising is this: you don't always have to spend money. You need to consider money and time when determining your ROI. It's no use saving £50 and spending five days on something else instead. Once you have a plan, look at the best way to execute it. Consider cost in money, your cost in time, achieving your objectives, business created, the cost of the business created, and your overall return. Just remember that giving discount codes is a good way to generate business, but you need to make sure that it's still worthwhile. I'll cover that in other chapters though.

Take home points:

1. Establish your target market and why they need your product or service
2. Create adverts that are relevant to your perfect client and what you are selling
3. Post your adverts in selected places where the right people will see them
4. Monitor your advertising success to establish what works best
5. Make sure that any discounts are viable and sustainable

Business Cost Management

Business costs can pile up quickly, especially as many suppliers charge ongoing monthly fees, some have annual fees, and then you have all the one-off payments too. You need to keep on top of this, especially when you start out and money is tight. Even when you're making money, you don't want to throw it away. Here are a few suggestions. Shop around. Make sure you're comparing apples with apples, so ask questions. If you need to make an investment in something you don't know an awful lot about, ask someone who does and do some research. I see so many businesses making quick and impulsive decisions, and then regretting them and paying twice as much to rectify the problem. Also, keep a record of what payments are due in the year, when they are due, and how much is due.

I strongly suggest putting the money aside before the payments are due. I have made many spreadsheets to track such expenses, and they are well worth it. I usually have most of my expenses (other than salaries) set aside a year in advance. So, when I start a new financial year, I've already set aside expenses such as accountant fees, website costs, insurances, subscriptions, etc. This way I don't have to scramble to find money when the bills come in. I then start setting aside for the next year, as money comes in. Planning and budgeting can eliminate some horrible surprises. When you have a small growing business you can keep on top of the expenses. When you have a large business, it may be worthwhile getting a specialist in to look at your expenses and bring them down. If you are buying stock and selling it, this becomes even more important, as your expenses are even greater. Consider using a procurement specialist, especially if they charge according to what they save you.

Also, looking ahead and planning what stock you may need, may help you to purchase the correct volume of stock too. There are supply chain specialists to help you with this, if you have a need. Business expenses can get out of control and eat up your profit. Not just for small businesses but larger ones too. There is no real one-size-fits-all approach to this, but just to say that you need to keep on top of this, and make sure you know what you're spending, why you're spending it, and that you're not overspending or wasting resources.

Take home points:

1. Do your research before taking on a business expense
2. Try and set aside the money for upcoming expenses
3. Monitor upcoming payments and what has been paid
4. Look at your supply chain so that you don't over or under stock

Business Plan

Most businesses start on passion and determination, without a hint of a business plan as it sounds intimidating and confusing. Most people only do a business plan if they need a loan and the bank insists on it. Here is my suggestion: if you need a business plan for a loan or investment, then ask what needs to be in a business plan and do one accordingly. If not, then think about your business and what you plan to do. This book has many different chapters; some will be relevant to you and some won't. So, sit down, determine what is relevant, and then come up with a plan. For example, what are you selling, who will need it, how will you get them to buy it, how much will you make, can you deliver what you promise, is it sustainable? These are the kinds of questions that you need to answer in a business plan. Why? Because without a plan you have no map to follow.

I see a business plan as important for two reasons (ignoring the need for a loan or investment). Firstly, so that you know what you are planning can work. Secondly, so that you can evaluate if you are achieving what you set out to do. Don't set a ten year plan at the start. You can if you like, but also set a six month plan. Decide what your overall goals are, what you want to achieve after six months, after one year, and then after five years. That way you can check after six months and see if you have done what you set out to do. What if the plan changes? I assume it will; no one gets it right from the start. This plan is not set in stone; it should change, but you still need it. If you have no plan to start with, how do you know to change it? My solution for a business plan is simple: don't copy someone else's template, do your own (unless you need it done specifically). Just make sure that you are clear where you are heading, and how you plan to get there. Review it regularly and adjust as needed. A business plan is not some catchy 'mission statement', it is an actual plan of what you want to do and how you plan to do it.

Take home points:

1. Have some sort of business plan, even if only a simple one
2. Review and adapt your business plan as you go along
3. Without a plan, you could drift with no direction
4. Make sure you are accountable to yourself with this plan
5. A business plan is an evolving document, and should always be relevant

As you can imagine, I make a lot of spreadsheets to monitor this kind of thing. I have seen many businesses get foreseeable expenses, like tax bills or stock bills of sorts, and it breaks them. Why did this happen? There could be many reasons, but it usually comes down to the fact that they were not prepared for the expense. If it was a foreseeable expense, that is probably not acceptable. What expenses do you foresee in the next twelve months? What income do you foresee? By putting these details down and doing some maths (or using a tool to do it for you), you can predict what to expect. Yes, this may not be exactly how it happens, but at least you can predict when you may have more disposable income, if needed.

For example, if you see that July is going to be tight, as you expect lower income in June, and higher expenses in July, then that is not a good time to buy new computers. This will help you to budget for upcoming expenses and make sure that you know when to spend money and, most importantly, it could reveal potential issues before they arise. If you purchase stock on ninety days credit and expect a flurry of sales in December, this means that three months later you can expect a hefty stock bill. If that happens to fall on the same month as a VAT bill, NI bill, and another unusual bill, you could be in trouble. This means you need to make sure that you don't spend all of the money made in December from all of the sales.

Many business owners see money in the bank and spend. Then the expenses come up, and they have no money. Don't do that; make sure you constantly are looking at least twelve months ahead, and budgeting as best you can. Another good idea is to compare these predictions with your actual figures (see the chapter on Financial Records for more about this). Not only to compare, but to help you to budget more accurately in the future. Also, if you have a template working the figures out, replacing predicted figures with actual figures will make the next predictions more accurate. This will keep you as prepared as you can be for upcoming expenses. Ask most businesses what their biggest problem is, and they will say cash flow. Get this right, and you'll be one step ahead.

Take home points:

1. Understanding upcoming expenses and expected income is vital
2. This may help you to see financial issues before they arise
3. Keep this up to date with as recent figures as possible
4. This should be a rolling document, so you're always looking ahead
5. Cash flow is one of the biggest issues with businesses, so you need to get this right

Creating a Brand

Believe it or not, this starts the day you start your business. This should filter through everything you do. Your advertising, marketing, the way you do business, even your behaviour and attire could all come down to a brand that you are building. The first step is to decide what that brand should be. Decide who you're trying to sell to, and what you're selling, as that would play a huge part in making this decision. Most people think that creating a brand is making a logo. That is surely part of it, but it's much bigger than that. Creating a logo may be one of the steps but, even before that, you need to know what your logo is there to achieve.

Let me tell you from experience: rebranding after years of trading is hard work. Your brochures, content, adverts, give-aways, marketing material, website, and everything else, will need to be updated. It is a lot of work. The more time you spend deciding your plan at the start, the more accurate your logo and proposed brand will be, and the less likely you will need to change it in the future. Think about the plan and make sure your logo fits in with that plan. Think about your advertising message, your prices, and your services or products. Do they all speak to your ideal client (there is a chapter about your ideal client)? It's no use trying to market your product as a high value product, with a cheap looking logo. The other way around is not helpful either, and will confuse potential clients. It is so important that all the aspects of your business work together. You are constantly sending messages to potential clients. Your logo, website, advertising, marketing, interaction on social media, telephone calls, meetings, the way you dress, how you react, how you reply to clients, how much you charge, what other add-on services you provide... it all comes down to your brand.

The logo is usually people's first stop on this journey because it's exciting and needs to be done early on. I would agree that it is exciting, but I do think that you need to consider the above before getting a logo created. Good designers will consider all of this and that is why their fees may seem high, because this takes time and effort. If you do your own logo, or simply give someone the idea to design it, you still need to consider all of this first. Once you have the logo done and have created some content, then you need to make sure that everything you do continues to build on the brand that you are creating. This journey never ends. You need to keep the message constant, so that clients and potential clients know who you are. That makes them more inclined to trust you and purchase what you are offering. Sending mixed messages with your brand can confuse people and send them away.

There are other things to consider when creating a logo, like if it will fit on your marketing materials, how it will look on documents, etc. If you're designing it yourself, these are questions to ask yourself. Remember that changing this logo down the line will be difficult, so try to get it right from the start.

Take home points:

1. Consider your target market, ideal client, and brand image before designing the logo
2. Rebranding can be costly, so getting this right from the start can be useful
3. Consider the colours and design of the logo and what the emotional response may be
4. Make sure your logo is consistent over all media
5. Making a logo is not just the design, it's about your brand and ambitions

Collaborations

These can be great, especially when your business is young and growing. However, you need to be careful when going into a collaboration. It's not quite as binding as starting a business with someone else, but you do need to go in with your eyes open. Does the other business owner share your views? Do they share your values? Are you comfortable being associated with them and their brand? Are you comfortable with them being associated with you and your brand? These are all things to consider, especially if you are doing joint marketing and advertising. I used to form collaborations with anyone; now I'm far more selective with whom I collaborate. I suggest you be the same way.

It's not just about sharing values and objective, but also about what both parties get out of it. If a collaboration is too one-sided, the other party may lose interest and the whole thing fails. I believe that a collaboration genuinely should provide value to both parties (as equally as possible) and provide the client with value greater than the sum of its parts. Let's say there is a local restaurant, who doesn't deliver, and a local delivery company. The restaurant will get more business if they deliver, and the delivery company will get more deliveries if they deliver food. That could be a win-win if they share values and objectives. You also need to consider the client experience if you're working closely with someone else. Like the example:

if the delivery service takes too long, the food may be cold and that may get you some negative reviews. You need to be clear on what you both need to do, and how it will help both parties. I think it needs to be worthwhile for both parties, otherwise someone will lose interest.

I also think that you both should treat the whole process as if it were your business reputation at stake, because it is. You need to consider the fact that they may drop the ball. How will you react if they do so? Keep this in mind, but the right strategic partnerships can be very helpful.

Take home points:

1. Very useful for small businesses and start-ups
2. Make sure you share the same ethics and ambitions as your collaborator
3. Make sure the partnership benefits both parties and the customer
4. Review the collaboration often and make sure it's still relevant
5. Make sure the parameters of the relationship are clear and followed

Data Analysis

This is one of my favourite topics, as I make spreadsheets, so this is right up my street. Most business owners have no idea what their data tells them, and this puts them at a disadvantage. If you understand what has happened, you can predict what will happen and take the right steps to see positive change. This applies to everything. Think about all the potential sources of data like social media sites, search engines, CRM solutions, websites, analytics, sales data, cost data, and any other relevant data that you can get your hands on. All of this has the potential of being analysed to tell a story. Your business may be unique, but there is always data to analyse and understand. If there isn't, you can always create data on which to analyse and report.

For example, if your client process is 5 steps long, which step is taking longer than it ought to? If you don't have that data, then can you track the client process? If so, now you have the data, so you can analyse it. I've seen people able to cut a two-hour process down to an hour and a half after collecting data, analysing it, and seeing the whole story. You may not think that's great, but when you're doing this four times a day, it is two hours. That's an extra client process per day which could mean a massive increase in profits! Efficient data analysis could reveal cost savings, potential for extra income, time savings, potential issues that need to be addressed, trends and flows, wasted effort, and many other useful insights for business owners. What you need to analyse will depend on what you need to know, and that will depend on your business.

I will say that if you are not analysing any data, you're not going to benefit from understanding it. I also find data analysis to be useful in making the right decisions. Say, for example, you're talking to a salesperson who is trying to convince you to advertise with them. They will give you all sorts of statistics and figures to convince you, like how many people will see your advert, and how many clicks you should get to your website. The big question is: will it make you money? More people seeing your advert may not be a good thing; you need the right people. You need to monitor what happens from the advert. Does it increase sales? Are they the right sales? Did it achieve its potential? No salesperson will tell you this, they just want to sell you the advertising space. You need to know if it works for you. This means getting the data. It may readily be available, or you may need to collect it yourself somehow and then analyse it to tell you what you want to know. Then you will have the information to make the right decisions.

Your need for data analysis will no doubt evolve as your business does, but it always should be on your mind. There is so much data available, and more on the way. Understanding this data, and what it means to you, is vital. It's not as scary as it sounds, and there are many people around who can help with this.

Online retail is an industry that heavily relies on data analysis. Who else is selling what you do? How much do they charge? What profit could you make if you set your selling prices to win the business? All of this comes down to data analysis and understanding what the data says.

Take home points:

1. There is so much data available, and you need to know what it says
2. If you don't have the right data to analyse, put processes in to capture what you need
3. Make sure you understand what you need to, so that you can make the right decisions
4. All data potentially could be analysed
5. Understanding this analysis could save you money or make you more productive

Dealing with Customers

This is done badly so often. Hopefully you will have lots of happy clients, but you may have the odd unhappy one. It is important that you deal with both properly. I think that the most important aspect of dealing with clients is simply managing their expectations. I don't know about you, but I get upset when I don't know what is happening. Let's look at a simple scenario. I buy something from you on Monday, and get an automated email saying that the item will be delivered on Wednesday. I am now expecting delivery. You then have a problem, as the stock you have is damaged, so you order new stock. The problem is that, despite your efforts, you'll now only be able to deliver on Thursday. Many business owners will not let the client know, as they don't want to let them down. Not telling them is letting them down even worse than disappointing them. A simple call on the Tuesday to let them know what has happened, and that their delivery will now be on Thursday, could solve the whole issue. Otherwise you could have an irate customer who took Wednesday off from work to wait for your delivery. Once that damage is done, it's hard to undo it, so keep the clients informed as soon as you can. This also applies to potential clients. When you are trying to win business, do you tell the potential clients what to expect? People have pre-conceived ideas of what you will provide them, and how you will do it, so actually telling them what to expect can leave them feeling at ease.

Even dealing with happy clients, a simple thank you or follow up can make a huge difference. I can't tell you how many times a follow up to a client has resulted in more work. A follow up is not just a courtesy, but also a good excuse to ask for a testimonial. A happy customer will say things about your business that you can't really get away with saying yourself. This could be very useful marketing content. I have found that many people won't send a testimonial unless you ask for it, but if you do ask they'll be happy to do so. As my dad used to say – If you don't ask, you don't get. Have a look at the chapter entitled Good & Bad Feedback too, as that is also relevant to dealing with people.

One last thing about customers: you don't have to keep them. If a customer is draining your resources, or being difficult to deal with, address it. Don't be rude, just let them know how things need to work, and ask them if they can do so, to keep the harmony. If they can't or won't, you can let them go. Just do it carefully so that it doesn't come back to bite you later. Always be respectful and factual. Personally, I would rather not have a difficult client if they are wasting my valuable time and not respecting me.

Take home points:

1. Always reply to clients, even if they are critical

2. Keeping clients informed throughout the process can eliminate needless issues
3. Notify clients immediately if changes occur
4. Always look to improve from customer feedback, however negative it may be
5. Ask happy customers for testimonials

Designing a Logo

This goes hand in hand with Creating a Brand, so see that chapter for more about this. Seeing as designing a logo is usually done early on, and it is the exciting part, let me make a few points about this. I used a simple logo creator when I started my business, and lived to regret it. After a few years of growth, I decided to change my logo. I had made a website, many advert pictures, marketing videos, demo videos, standard spreadsheets, PDF brochures, templates, business listings, free downloads, and branded gifts. It all needed to be changed when I rebranded. I do not want to do that again, nor do I wish it on you. If the first logo you design lasts you a lifetime, you'll save a lot of work. You don't really have to change old content, but you do need to change all the current content and, depending on what you do, that may be a huge task.

So, what do you need to consider when making a logo? When I created the first logo, I liked a design and colour and simply went for it. No thought about anything. When I made the second logo, here's what I considered. I thought about to whom I was selling and what would appeal to them. I thought about what emotions the colours would stir up (yes, that's a thing). I thought about how the logo would look on all the content that I would create, as well as all the documents. I thought about what it said about my brand and what messages it relayed. It involved way more thinking than just, "Oh, that looks nice". Now I realise that this may be overwhelming to think about when you're starting, and you may not be able to afford to get this professionally done, but at least give it some thought. The more you get right here, the longer the logo could last you and it may only need minor tweaks in the future. You may not get this 100% right, but you can at least get it better than I did on the first go. Don't get too bogged down with this, but spend some time thinking about it. Maybe make a few options and put them out for others to tell you what the logos 'say' to them. This may help you to see if you're on the right track.

Take home points:

1. Designing a logo is more than just making the logo, it requires thought
2. The logo will be the centre point for your entire brand
3. Make sure it's relevant to your target market and what you are selling
4. The more thought you put into this, the longer it should last you
5. Rebranding is a costly exercise; try and get this right from the start

Email Newsletters

Depending on who you ask, this can be a great marketing tool or a complete waste of time. I think much of the success of email newsletters comes down to two things. What you put in them, and how often you send them. When you start out in business there is so much to do and you're all excited, so you end up doing everything that you can. The more I went on in business, the more I realised what worked and what didn't, so I could do more of what did work, and less of what didn't. Starting an email newsletter is like getting a pet. It's a long-term responsibility and it will require work. If you simply start a newsletter because 'that's what you do', then no doubt it will fizzle out. The other problem is that after six months you start to run out of content ideas, and you realise that designing a newsletter each month takes time and effort. That's if you send it monthly. If you send it more often than that it's even harder and, if you send it less frequently, it can lose its effect.

Before you start an email newsletter, here are a few things to consider. Who is it designed for? Will the layout be the same each time, just with different content? How often will you send it? What will it contain? What do you want to achieve with it? All of these will help you to know whether or not you can keep this up, and it will also help you to be open and honest with the readers upfront in what they can expect from your newsletter. If you ask them to sign up for vouchers and then just do advertising, you will lose their trust. If you tell them what to expect, and when to expect it, then you need to deliver what you have said.

It can take a while to build lists of people who have signed up, so you need to be disciplined with this, even when you are busy or when you lack ideas to write about. Trust me, I know. You also need to monitor the success of the newsletters. Are you getting sales from them? Are they achieving what you want? If not, do you need to change them or are they worth doing at all? If something isn't working then it needs to be changed or dropped, as it's no use flogging a dead horse. Have a look at the chapter entitled Data Analysis about analysing data, but this is ideal for such analysis. If you're not serious about your email newsletter it will most likely fail, so this is one of those things that you need to do properly or not at all. It's no use wasting valuable time and resources on this if you're not going to get the return that you need. If you're time-poor and cash-rich, I'd suggest outsourcing this to a virtual assistant or email newsletter professional.

As I said, at the start of this chapter, this could be very useful to you or it could fail miserably and waste your time. It takes time and good content to grow a following but, once you have that following, you have an audience which is hard to create anywhere else. The rewards can be huge, but the investment (money or time) is costly. If you do an email newsletter, make sure you know what you're in for, and be prepared for the long haul.

Take home points:

1. An email newsletter is a long-term investment of time and, potentially, money
2. This is not a quick win and should be taken seriously, if done at all
3. Keep your content relevant to your readers and potential clients
4. Try and have a consistent template, to make it easier to create each newsletter
5. Promise what you plan to deliver, and then deliver what you promise

Financial Records

This is not really a suggestion, but a requirement. You need to keep a record of all your financial transactions. So, how do you do this? I would strongly suggest asking your accountant about this. You may end up outsourcing this whole aspect to your accountant but, if you do it yourself, I'd strongly suggest chatting to your accountant. Up to this point I've always done my own financial records, so that I am 100% in control and know what is happening. I am ultimately responsible, as a business owner, so I like to be in control of this. I did however talk to my accountant so that they knew what to expect from me. I didn't want to do one thing, and then they had to double up the work to do my year end accounts.

I made changes to my records to serve two purposes. One, they told me what I wanted to know while running my business and, two, they were also in the right format for my accountant. This means that I know what is happening and the accountant's effort is minimal. This whole process is getting easier with modern software, but you both still need to be on the same page. Often accounting software is set up for accountants and it leaves you, as the business owner, in the dark and completely reliant on the accountant. This may suit them, but it shouldn't work for you. Whatever bookkeeping and accounting plan you decide on, you need to have the relevant information as you need it, it needs to provide your accountant with what they need as they need it, and it needs to be legally compliant with the government. These laws obviously change, so that's why it's good to have a good accountant and to chat to them about this.

Take home points:

1. Make sure you and your accountant are on the same page
2. Make sure you are in control of your finances and understand your position
3. Keep accurate and up to date records
4. Make sure your records are compliant with the law
5. Put double checks in place to monitor these figures

Good & Bad Feedback

As the world moves more online, we now have a new set of people to contend with. Those that comment or post about our businesses, whether they are clients or not. How do we deal with them? I think each case needs to be addressed individually, but here are some suggestions that I have learned. Don't ignore genuine praise or criticism. If someone is saying good things about your business or products, at very least like it or comment and say thanks. It will make a huge difference to that client, and a happy client is your best form of marketing. Then there are negative comments and reviews. What do you do about them? Again, this will depend on the comment, but here are some suggestions.

If it is a genuine customer, don't argue with them. Your immediate response may be an emotional one, and they may not have reacted in the best way because they may be upset. You need to address it, see their point of view, and react respectfully. You may need to set them straight if they have misquoted facts, but be careful how you do that and don't use it as an excuse. Try and see it from their point of view and respond to the issue, not the emotion. You can say something like, "Thank you for letting us know that your delivery was late. We're very sorry that this has upset you, so please accept this 20% voucher off your next order". They may have called you useless, or said other untrue things, but you don't want to be the business that argues with clients, especially on a social media platform. Try and listen to the actual problem and don't take offence by the emotional add-ons. In the above example you're apologising for being late and not getting upset because they called you useless. Even if they say you were a week late and you were only twenty-four hours late. Perhaps you can correct them, but don't argue; still apologise for being late.

There are times where people are completely abusive. I would say call them out, but do it without retaliating. You need to keep your nose clean, because other customers are seeing this. Don't stoop to their level. If the person bad-mouthing you was never a client (it happens) you could simply ask them what they purchased (as you don't recall them having done so) and what they would like to see improved. I did this and, as you can imagine, I got no reply. The comment was never deleted (although I contested it) but now at least future clients can see the comment and can determine that it was fake, given my response and their lack of follow up comment. I didn't attack them or accuse them of lying, I simply asked what I could do. Stick to the high road and remain professional; let them sink to the bottom. Others will see that and respect you for it.

One last thing I will say about this is to look at all criticism, however aggressive it may be. Someone may be particularly aggressive and say completely unfair things but, in amongst that, there is one fact that you can improve on. Don't throw out the one good fact with all the abuse. Look carefully at what they are saying and ask yourself two simple questions: what can I learn from this, and how can I improve? If you can learn one thing to make you future client relations better, do it. Even if it comes from an unreasonable rant. Have a look at the chapter entitled Dealing with Customers for more about this.

Take home points:

1. Don't ignore genuine praise or criticism
2. Remain professional with your responses, especially the ones to negative comments
3. Learn what you can from criticism, however rude it may be, to improve your business
4. Deal with spam messages if you can't get them removed
5. Remember that others can often see your comments, and they may be potential clients

Hiring Staff

I'm not going to say too much about hiring staff, because I never have (for my own business) and I don't plan to. I have, however, done many spreadsheets for the HR (Human Resources) industry, so have dealt with some excellent HR professionals. I have learned from them and from what I have seen some employers do, so here are my suggestions. I believe that the biggest jump in hiring staff is hiring the first staff member. If you have 127 staff and hire the 128th, you've done it all before and have the infrastructure in place. When you hire your first staff member I will assume that you have no experience at it, and that you don't know what to do.

Firstly, there are many HR professionals around who work with smaller companies, so my suggestion is simple. Talk to one of them before you hire someone. In fact, talk to one of them before you even start advertising for the role. As soon as you decide to hire someone, the next step should be to contact an HR person. When it comes to HR, you are dealing with people. You are also dealing with people who could make or break your business. You're dealing with potential law suits, and you're dealing with people who could take your business to the next level. You must get this right. Yes, it is going to be expensive. Yes, it will cost you more than just the new salary. The other downside is that your workload won't decrease the second you hire the new person, it will actually increase, because you need to train the new person and get them up to speed with the way you do things.

When it comes to hiring your first staff member, I have a theory. This may not work, depending on your situation, but it's worth considering. In another chapter I talk about Outsourcing Work, where you contract work out to a freelancer or business instead of employing someone. This may be a good first step. Here's my thought behind this. Outsourcing work is more flexible. You can get a few hours done per day, pay per project, or pay as you go. You don't need to find enough work for someone working for you. You also have the flexibility to stop if the work dries up. Yes, you'll pay more per hour, but you have the flexibility to adapt the scope of work. Then, when you see that the work has been constant, and the flow is there, you can use your experience to lay out a job description. You now know what works needs to be done, you have an idea of how it should be done, and you've hopefully ironed out all the issues. I believe that you would now be in a much better place to chat to an HR advisor and hire your first employee. You've also been spending money by outsourcing the work, so the salary payments don't come as a financial shock. In fact, if the staff member comes in at the same number of hours required, you may even save some money. Once you have your first employee, you can then grow from there.

The other aspect of HR is that you are dealing with human beings. I see HR as being three-sided: what you want, what they want, and what the law says. You really want those three things to line up, that's why it's so important to talk to an advisor. Firstly, you need to get what you want to line up with the law, and then you need to find the right person who has the same objectives as you. This can be hard, so you need all the advice you can get. I haven't even mentioned all of the legal requirements for hiring staff, but these change all the time and I'm not an HR specialist. Here is another reason to talk to someone before employing anyone. If you want to grow your business beyond yourself, you'll more than likely need to employ someone at some stage. This is a good thing, but it needs to be done properly, so please make sure you get the right advice.

Take home points:

1. Get professional advice before employing people
2. Possibly outsource work to get a streamlined process before employing
3. Make sure your employment is legal and done properly
4. Remember that you are dealing with people, make sure your objectives match theirs
5. This may be one of the biggest decisions you make, spend time and thought on it

I don't know about you, but I hate insurances until I need them. Most of them you just pay, pay, pay, and never get anything back. The problem is that if you need them and don't have them, the consequences can be devastating. When I started my business, I started looking for the insurances that I needed, and found two that I required. I approached a local insurance company and they sold me what I asked for (which I had found via some internet searches). I went on for a few years until I met another insurance broker and got a like-for-like quote. They then asked me why I had those policies and they explained what the policies were both for. As it turned out, I was over-insured in one, and under-insured in the other.

The insurance broker explained that they were not allowed to advise what insurances you needed (to stop people from manipulating you, I suppose) and people were getting the wrong policies because no one could advise them. The advisor simply explained to me what both of the policies covered in respect to my business. I saw straight away that I was incorrectly insured, so I changed the policies (which saved me some money). When it comes to insurances, you need to find out what you need. Call a broker, explain your business to them, and ask them what policies may be relevant. Then ask them to explain what those policies will cover, how they work and how they relate to your business. Then make the decision that is best for you.

Some insurance salespeople are less than honest, so you need to shop around. There are some excellent brokers out there, so ask other business owners in similar fields for referrals. In fact, I see many business owners asking others what insurances they have, to get an idea of what may be required. Unfortunately, things like insurances are necessary, so make sure you have the right policies in place.

Take home points:

1. Establish what insurances you'll need in your industry
2. Research the insurances to find out what is best for you
3. Ask questions and compare like-for-like products for price savings
4. Make sure that you are adequately insured, not over or under insured
5. Don't be scared to shop around at renewal time, it could save you money

Invoices

Believe it or not, there are legal requirements as to what needs to be on an invoice. This is something that you need to get sorted out early on. In fact, I had this done before I even started on my website or told anyone about my business. I have seen so many people ask how to make an invoice after the work was done and the client asked for an invoice. I will go more into this in the chapter called Processes and Procedures, but I wanted to highlight the invoice. The first thing you need to do is chat to your accountant and see what bookkeeping option you need to use. Many programs will have invoicing built in, so you will already have the template. These still need to be set up for your business, depending on how it is set up. I would strongly advise looking at the government's website and making sure that your invoice has all the details they have asked for. "My accountant didn't tell me", is not an excuse, as far as the tax man is concerned.

My other advice would be to keep on top of what invoices have been sent, what invoices need to be sent, and what's been paid. Invoice payments are your lifeline, and you need to know what is going on with all of them. Make sure that you know - your accountant knowing is not good enough, unless they follow up for payments. My last bit of advice for invoices is to be clear on your payment terms. So many people use a template for an invoice and forget to put payment terms on it, and then have an uphill battle when the client doesn't pay. Make it clear, make sure the client knows, and make sure you follow up when you need to. In my experience, the longer an invoice is overdue, the less likely they will pay.

Take home points:

1. Find out what needs to be on an invoice, legally
2. Chat to your accountant to make sure you're compliant
3. Keep track of issued invoices and follow up when you need to
4. Make sure you have payment terms clearly displayed
5. You are responsible for the invoice details, no one else

This is a massive topic, and I could probably write a whole book on this, but I'll try and keep this short and relevant. Let's start with hardware. Most start-ups don't have the budget for fancy technology, and it may only be you with your laptop at home, so you can probably keep the costs down with regards to hardware. I will say this, though: when you are hard at work and you sit waiting for your computer to think about what it's doing, it is incredibly frustrating. If you can spend a little extra when buying a computer, go for something with a slightly higher specification. The higher the specification, the longer it should last, and the less stressed you will be while waiting for it. Salespeople may try and get you to spend more money on design, functionality, or brands that you don't need. I'd rather spend it on a more powerful computer. Once you know what you want, shop around, you'll be surprised how much money you can save.

When it comes to software, I am biased because I prefer spreadsheets to just about anything else. I like them because I can make what I need. I can make a software solution that revolves around my business, and not try to squash my business into a ready-made software solution. The more we become reliant on computers, the more software will become available, and the more we'll need it. You will need software for your business, but it's important that you think about what you need before buying anything. Is there a ready-made, cost effective solution that does exactly what you want? If so, that may be the solution.

If not, then you have a choice of four main options. 1. Find something somewhat suitable and adapt your business to fit the software. 2. Get software custom made, which can be ridiculously expensive and unaffordable to most businesses. 3. Buy a customisable solution and get it customised for what you need (which could also be quite expensive). 4. Get something made using an existing tool, like a spreadsheet. Many people who come to me have already ruled out points 1 to 3, as they are just not viable in many cases. You need to make the decision that is right for you. If you ask three different IT professionals the same question about what software to use, don't be surprised if you get three different answers. We all have different opinions and ideas about this. You need to ask some questions, do some research, and get what is right for your business. You need to find the balance of what you want the software to do, what the ready-made options already do, and how much you can afford to pay.

One last thing I will say about IT hardware and software is about security and compliance. This is an area that is changing almost daily, so it's pointless saying anything other than make sure you address this. Check what security measures you need to put in place and stick to them. Also, check what the laws are relating to data management and storage. In 2018 there was an addition of GDPR rules, which was all about how data is stored and processed. It would be very wise to familiarise yourself with this, to be compliant. Sometimes it makes sense to use established storage solutions who do much of the compliance work for you, but that doesn't exclude you from your responsibilities. IT can be an overwhelming subject, because there is so much to know. It is one of those areas where you need to get the basics right first. Yes, people may try and sell you unnecessary stuff, like with anything else, but find someone you trust and get their advice.

Take home points:

1. Get the right specs on your hardware; spend on performance over gimmicks
2. Look at all software options, depending on price and requirements
3. Don't be scared to use things like custom spreadsheets to keep costs down
4. Make sure that your data is secure, and you have been compliant with any laws
5. Have a go-to IT support person, in case things go wrong

Lead Reminders

Why is this chapter in here? I'll tell you why. I've made hundreds, if not thousands, of spreadsheets in my life, but the one that has single-handedly brought in the most money was one to remind me to follow up leads. If you're selling low cost items online or in a store this may not apply to you, but if you are selling high cost items to people in person, then this is a must. I found that so many people would say they were interested in what I had to offer, and then they would disappear. They would get bogged down with work and forget. Or someone would refer someone else, and they would then not get back to me. I didn't want to add loads of cold leads into my CRM, but I did want to make a note of them, so I made a spreadsheet to do so. I then periodically followed up with each lead and made a note of the date, so I knew when next to chase them. So many of those leads eventually bought something, and I suspect many would not have, if I didn't follow up.

People don't always buy straight away, sometimes they need time to decide. If you forget about them, they may well forget about you. I'm not talking about hassling them to buy, just a gentle reminder every so often, so that they don't forget about you. If you have people showing interest in what you do, and then going quiet, get yourself a list like this. Hunt me down and see what I have available, if you'd prefer a spreadsheet, but get a list going. Check it regularly and keep it up to date. You'll be surprised how many go from cold leads to paying clients. You'll thank me later. People spend a fortune for good leads, and this list is like a free list of actual people who have already expressed an interest in purchasing your product or service. This is like gold dust, and I'm surprised that many businesses who could have a list like this, simply don't.

Take home points:

1. Interested potential customers may take a while to decide to buy, don't forget them
2. Keep a list of follow-ups and follow up as you need to
3. Track which follow-up leads become clients, you'll be surprised
4. Check the list regularly so you don't forget about anyone
5. This could be a gold mine if done correctly

Legal Requirements

This is one of the most boring and annoying parts of a business but, unfortunately, the part that could get you into the most trouble if you ignore it. You need to find out what legal requirements you need to undertake. For example, are there any requirements for your industry? That's a good place to start. Then look at all the aspects of your business like your website, data storage, process terms and conditions, and staff contracts. All of these will require legal paperwork, and they (and others) will all need to be addressed. Most people just copy someone else's template, which is possibly the worst thing to do, as your business is not like theirs. You can either pay someone to do this for you, or you can do your own contracts. Whatever you decide, you need to make sure they are valid for your business and that they are correct.

I will suggest that, if possible, speak to the right person for each legal document. For example, when GDPR hit in 2018 there was a mad panic for GDPR policies for people's websites. People were asking other people for theirs to copy, and it was chaos. I simply went to the ICO's website (those enforcing GDPR) and signed up. I then received the right templates to adapt for my business, with instructions on how to do so. If you can get your information straight from the source, then do so, otherwise get advice from people who know. Asking people who are just as clueless as you, and accepting their best guess, is not advisable when it comes to legal requirements. Nowadays, with so many legal issues, you almost need to look at everything you do and ask the question, “Are there any legal requirements for this?”. Unfortunately, not knowing about the law is not an excuse, you need to make it your business to know.

Take home points:

1. Make sure you know what is required
2. Don’t just copy other legal documents from competitors
3. Try and get the requirements from the source, if possible
4. Consult a legal professional, or do it yourself, but get it done
5. You are ultimately responsible, so make sure you understand what has been done

Limited Company v Sole Trader

This is one of the first questions that you should ask your accountant. The rules are changing constantly and there are so many things to consider, that it's pointless writing down all the parameters. The reason why this is so important to do at the start, is that so much depends on this. For example, if you're a sole trader, you may just use your name. Then, after three years, you start to grow and want to take on other staff. Now you want to change your company name and start a new brand. Now you need a new logo, a new name, a new website and domain, all new branding, and a new start in many aspects. If your plan always was to grow to this level, then it may have been better to have started as a limited company and get all the other aspects sorted out around that. If your plan is always to work by yourself, then being a sole trader may bring some benefits, like easier tax reports and possibly a savings in tax.

This is the reason why it's best to talk to your accountant and decide what is best for you, based on your business and plans. When I started Spreadsheet Solutions, I decided to go straight into having a limited company, because I knew the plan was for my wife to come on board. I probably could have saved money at the start by being a sole trader, but the change-over would have been a costly pain, so I went with the future-proof plan from the start. Think about where you want to take the business, chat to your accountant to see what will be best for you, and then make the decision.

Take home points:

1. Decide this early on
2. Make this decision not only on what you plan to do now, but how you plan to grow
3. Consult an accountant about which option is best for you
4. Consider potential growth and future name changes when deciding
5. This is reversable, but could cost you if you change too often

Marketing

Marketing is one aspect of business that I grossly underestimated but, once I learned about it, I discovered that actually it's not as hard as it looks. That may sound like an odd statement to make, but hear me out on this. Before starting my business, marketing sounded easy to me. Make some adverts, post some posts, and whack your logo on them; how hard can it be? Well, the answer is much harder than that. Marketing is part of everything that you do. From the high-profile advertising campaign to the reply email that people get when they sign up to your email newsletter, that is all marketing. What message are you putting across? Are you sending mixed messages? Do they all accurately represent your brand? These are all considerations to be made. You also need to make your advertising appeal to your ideal client. Do you even know who's your ideal client? Have a look at the chapter entitled Target Audience to find out more about this. You need to have someone in mind when you create marketing content.

If you're in retail, advertising may be as simple as a picture of your product and a price. Marketing, however, is a whole other beast. This is about deliberately growing your brand and appealing to your target audience, for them to realise why they want to purchase what you're selling. Often, you're not only selling a service or product, but an idea or emotion. You're selling a solution to a problem which is causing them pain of some sort. Getting that point across requires good and accurate marketing. That is what I found so hard, as I am a straight-down-the-line, say-it-as-it-is, take-it-or-leave-it, kind of guy. If you're like me, try and put yourself in your client's shoes and ask yourself what they are feeling. What do they need? Now provide them with that. Your marketing should also fit with your brand. If your brand is serious and professional, your marketing should follow suit. Perhaps the odd campaign may differ, to make a point or get people's attention, but you need to keep your brand and also target audience in mind when marketing.

One of the most helpful things I found with advertising and marketing was the analytics. I love analysing data with spreadsheets, so I was all over this from the start, and it helped me greatly. I monitored every campaign down to each post on each site or email newsletter, and all the clicks back to the website. I also monitored where my business was coming from. Remember, marketing is not only your adverts, but even comments and posts that you as a business owner make. I've probably got more business in through personal messages than I have from adverts. The analytics from these posts helped me to see what was working and what wasn't. So much so, that some of the campaigns I was most excited about failed miserably. Others which I thought of on the spur of the moment, and just ran with them, went on to be tremendously successful. I then adjusted future campaigns, based on what I had learned.

Some of the failures came from me copying business-to-client, when I was business-to-business, and others just didn't work for my brand. Either way, I learned from them. When campaigns did work, I asked why, and then tried to use that again in the next campaign. Advertising and marketing take up a lot of time, and it feels like you're just throwing content at a wall and hoping some will stick. If you know what's worked and what hasn't, it means that you can start to throw the right content properly and have more stick. It also makes it more exciting when you know how your campaigns have performed and this gives you energy and enthusiasm for the next one.

Take home points:

1. Marketing is part of everything you do
2. Make your marketing appeal to your ideal client
3. Your marketing should fit with your brand
4. Make sure you track your marketing success
5. Learn from mistakes and constantly look to improve

When most people become business owners, they are almost forced into face-to-face or online networking. I am a huge advocate of this, as I think it is extremely helpful, but there are some things to consider. What do you want to get out of networking? If it's sales, then listen to this carefully. If you go to a networking event to sell, you will probably be disappointed. Why do I go? To form relationships and meet people in the same boat as me. To let them know what I can provide, so that they know when to refer me. To build trust and have some human interaction - having your own business can be a lonely place. To show myself as an expert in what I do. I don't go to sell, but if I do all these things correctly, I will sell. If you sell to the people in the room, your sales are limited. If you get the people in the room to understand what you offer, and to trust you, they will refer you and those sales are unlimited.

Another trick that I learned when meeting someone for the first time at a networking event: let them talk first. This gives you an opportunity to hear what they do, so you can tailor your response based on what they do. Also, it makes them feel good and looks like you are not in a rush to sell yourself. There is a downside to networking like this. It can be exhausting. What's more, is that it can take up all your time if you're not careful. If you search all the networking events near you and online, and you try to attend them all, you could become a full-time networker. There are also many different types of events. Some weekly, some monthly, some periodically, and some annually. They all have advantages and disadvantages, and they all need to be approached differently. A weekly event is about building relationships and getting and giving referrals. An annual event is about meeting new people. A speed networking event is about making contacts to follow up with.

The approach to each networking event is different. Go to the event with a plan and make sure that the plan suits the structure of the event. Once again, like with all advertising and marketing: keep a record of what these events cost you in time and money, and then see how much business they bring in. At the end of the day this is about business and, if you're not getting an adequate return on your time and money investment, you may need to switch events or at least tactics. Yes, you'll still make friends and interact with people wherever you go, but personally I would rather go to events that help generate the most business.

Take home points:

1. Don't go networking to sell to the room, get to know the room instead
2. Show yourself as an approachable expert, so that people can refer you to others

3. Be quick to listen and slow to talk
4. Pick the events carefully and approach each one with a plan
5. Analyse the success and adapt as necessary

Outsourcing Work

I spoke about this in the chapter entitled Hiring Staff, as outsourcing work can be an excellent way to determine the scope of the work and get used to paying for it, before employing someone to do the work. Outsourcing doesn't only have to be a precursor to employing someone, it can make sense at any stage of your business growth. So, why would you outsource work when you can do it yourself? Good question. I think there needs to be a balance between time, money, and what you want to achieve by doing the work. As an example, let's say that you needed to get a spreadsheet made for your business, and you kind of know your way around Excel. You have loads of time because you're not busy, you have no money because you have no work yet, and you don't need much from the spreadsheet. If you can handle it, and you can't afford to pay for it, then it makes sense to do it yourself. Fast forward a few years, and now you need a better spreadsheet to do more. You have more money, because you're busy, and therefore you have no time. Now it makes more sense to outsource the task of making the spreadsheet to someone like me, so that you can spend your valuable time doing what you are good at and need to do. Also, you're likely to get a better product from a professional than you can make yourself.

There are other times when you need something and have no idea how to do it, so you need to outsource the work. You probably still will have the option of a cheaper outsource, so you still need to balance quality with price. The bottom line is that if you're running a successful business, the chance of you being able to do everything is unlikely. You can either employ staff, which is a more permanent deal, or you can outsource work. Yes, outsourcing potentially may cost more per hour, but you are not committed, nor do you have to use up all the hours (unless you're on a retainer). Personally, I think that as soon as you can afford to start outsourcing, you probably should. If you're too busy, you're not productive. You need to be focussing on whatever it is you do that earns money. Anything else that takes up your time could be outsourced, and often at a lower rate than what you're earning (if you're working flat out). Your time often can be better used elsewhere to get the money in. Let someone else do the work that you're not even that interested in anyway.

There are even times when outsourcing can help you take a break or holiday; there are no rules with this. There was one thing I did notice. If you outsource work and then sit around doing nothing, it can play on your mind that you could have done that and saved money. My advice is to outsource work when you are busy, so that you are being productive, and then you can justify that spending in your own mind. If you're now wondering to whom you can outsource work, connect with people in person and on social media and get to know them. Many are helpful, and you can probably find someone to outsource just about any work to.

Take home points:

1. Find the balance between time, money, and quality of work
2. If you're getting busy, outsource the work you don't need to do
3. If you're cash poor and time rich, maybe do the work yourself unless you can't
4. Outsourcing is a good initial alternative to employing staff
5. Connect with people to build a network of potential outsourcing opportunities

Pricing

This is probably single-handedly the most important issue to address when starting a business. I often see questions, on social media, asking how much people should charge. You then get a chorus of, "Charge what you're worth", which means nothing because you can never charge what you're worth. I've also seen people doing business for a year, being busy, and then the accountant tells them that they haven't made any money. Why? Because they weren't charging enough.

So, how do you calculate prices? This can be a complicated process, depending on what you're selling, and I have made many custom spreadsheets to calculate selling prices. I can't give you an accurate formula, without knowing what you do, but here are some things for which you need to look out. You need to consider all your costs. Not just stock costs (if you have them) but all costs. Your time, postage and packaging (P&P), payment fees, platform fees, storage costs, advertising and marketing costs, taxes, and any other costs that may be relevant to what you are selling. So many people take the cost price and add a margin. That's easy to do, but does your margin cover your costs and give you a profit? You're also then swayed by what others are charging and what you think the market expects to pay for what you are selling. That all plays a part in your pricing. It's no use working yourself half to death so that you can end up making no money. You need to get the pricing right and the sooner, the better. My suggestion would be to do the following. Firstly, make a list of all your costs, including the time that processing each order will take you. Include all P&P and any other fees that you may pay, such as platform fees or payment fees. If you put the item in a packet to give to the client, cost in the price of the packet. Everything. Now you need to look at how many products you plan to sell. Some people may only need to sell one high-priced item per month, others may need to sell many low-priced items per day. Look at what you need to sell and what you can sustain over a long period. Look at your average sales per month. Now look at your advertising and marketing budget, including any other overheads that you want to include here. Take the monthly cost, divide that by the number of products you plan to sell per month, and then add that figure to the cost price. Now decide what your margin needs to be. I would suggest talking to your accountant about this as they can advise, based on your overheads and tax liabilities. Any expenses that you haven't already considered need to be considered here. You can then calculate what you will charge for each item.

Now go and look at the market. What are others charging and how do you compare? If you're more expensive, that's not necessarily the end of the world, but you may have to appeal to a different target market. This will then affect your brand creation, marketing, and advertising. Do you see how this all fits together? If the worst comes to the worst, and you realise that what you want to sell won't make you enough money, at least you've figured it out before flogging a dead horse for a year. Because of my personality, the above came naturally for me; it was common sense to do this. I realise that many others are not wired this way, so this will be a massive headache for you. Talk to someone. Chat to your accountant, or someone who knows about prices and figures, and go through the whole process. Look at all the costs and how much money realistically you will make, and then decide on prices. If you need to position yourself differently in the market, do so. That's why branded products are more expensive than no-name brands, and yet they still sell. You can do that too if you get your advertising, marketing, and brand awareness done well.

The other thing to consider with pricing is when you will offer a discount. Please make sure that your discount is also considered. So many businesses lose out on money when offering a discount. Now that may be the plan short term, but do things like this with a clear understanding of the consequences rather than just on a whim.

Take home points:

1. Consider all costs when pricing, not just the big ones

2. Work out what you need to charge before comparing with competitors' prices
3. Adjust your marketing and advertising if you need to charge more
4. Make sure that your margin includes all overhead costs and your profit
5. If you're not sure your price will make you money, ask for help

You may not find this hard to believe, but I had many of the processes and procedures set for my business before I even had a live website. I am very process-driven, but most people are not. If you are, then this chapter may not be relevant to you. If you're not, you're going to want to think about this. Processes and procedures sound like boring corporate meetings and massive documents that no-one reads, but they are more than that. They are, very simply, the process in which you do your work. When you start out in business, you tend to want to get going and start selling, but you need to think about this. Think about the process from start to finish. When you get the first sale, what will that look like? How will it go? Walk through the process of someone first hearing about your business, to the point where they write you a raving review and you thank them (and even beyond). Plan that process, think about it, and ask yourself what you would do if things went off course at any stage. Make sure you have the right tools, templates, answers, and solutions for any eventuality that you can think of.

These will change over time, so you won't get them 100% at the start, but so many new business owners don't even consider this at all. For example, if someone asks if they can return a product, what is your returns policy? If you haven't got one, scrambling to get one at this stage would be unprofessional. Getting your processes and procedures sorted out early on makes the whole process easier when you need them. I've seen people do work for other businesses and, upon request for an invoice, they ask what an invoice needs to look like. This should have been done before the work was taken on because, if you didn't plan to invoice for it, why were you doing it? This is an obvious requirement, but some processes are not so obvious. You don't only need to look at the obvious processes, but also the 'what if' processes. What if things go wrong? These processes are often harder to predict, but often the client is in a less-than-forgiving mood when things go wrong, so you need to be ready.

Processes and procedures go further than just the client journey; they apply to all aspects of business. Employing staff, doing accounts, internal auditing, advertising and marketing, social media, tax, legal obligations, and all other aspects of business need processes. You don't need to have a manual on each, but a clear idea of what you need and how to do each task. I usually think of each thing I do and then think how I would pass the job onto someone else. I then make the right templates and tools to do what needs to be done quickly and efficiently. I then use the required tools myself and set reminders and notes. This means that I am more organised. It also means that I know what to do, and have the right tools, so I can do things quicker and with fewer errors. If I do need to pass the task on to someone else one day (staff member or outsourcing) I already have a plan and process to follow, which makes their job easier.

Take home points:

1. Think about what process each aspect of your business follows
2. Plan for the unexpected, especially for the customer journey
3. You don't need to go overboard, but have the templates that you will need
4. Get your processes in order, to make you more efficient and reduce errors
5. The more organised you are, the easier it will be to hand over tasks to others

Should you show prices on your website or get people to request quotes? This is a question that I have seen asked many times and debated to the full. There are almost always two sides to this argument. The first side says to be as transparent as possible, by displaying your prices, and the other side says to get people hooked before telling them the price as they are more likely to buy. Let's start with those who are selling a product or package service that is pre-priced. I would say to you that you need to show your prices. The only exemption to this would be if you're so high-end, you're going for an if-you-have-to-ask-you-probably-can't-afford-it approach. For anybody selling to anyone who is not stinking rich, I'd advise having some prices.

The other group who can't display prices are the businesses who provide tailor-made solutions. You can't quote until you know what is required, and only then can you calculate a price. I fell firmly into that category, with the custom spreadsheets that I offer. I couldn't give prices unless I did a quote, based on the individual requirements. So, what did I do? There were a few things which I found made people more likely to approach me. I gave a price range on the website. I had a whole section explaining what the process would be like, starting from when they first made contact. I gave them a price range (it was a large range, but at least it gave some idea), I told them roughly how long it would take (still a range), and told them roughly what process I would follow. Anyone who wanted to know what they were in for, could read that and know exactly what to expect. My reasoning behind that was simple, it served a few purposes. The first was a question I asked myself: would I request a quotation if I had no idea what it would cost? I'm not sure I would. We are often hounded by businesses and pressured by salespeople once they get our name and contact details, so I was hesitant to ask for a quote even if I was interested. I didn't want this to put people off asking me for a quote. I also thought about me selling the product. What if someone asks for a quote and sends me all the details? I then spend hours or days drawing up a comprehensive quote for £1,000.00 and they are shocked, as they expected it to be £50.00. I've now wasted that time, they think I'm expensive, and I've got nothing from it. If I had given a price range of £500.00 to £1,500.00, they never would have wasted my time in the first place. I didn't want to be spending time doing unnecessary quotes. In fact, I even go as far as to drop a ballpark figure into the initial conversation, if I can, before I even draw up the quote. This means that I get in a very large percentage of my quotes, as I have already weeded out the 'tire kickers'.

Some business owners charge for quotes and then deduct the price if they accept the job. You may need to do this if the quote takes time and you find you're getting time wasters. However, if you do so, make sure that you give good solid guidelines before quoting. It's wrong to keep people in the dark, charge for a quote, and then hit them with an unrealistic price. I think the basic question to ask yourself, when it comes to showing prices and quoting, is one which you should ask yourself in life in general. How would I want others to treat me? Now treat them the same way. I've heard people say to me that they don't show prices because theirs are more expensive, and they need to show the client why. They say that their product or service is superior, and they want to show that to their clients, so they don't display prices or people will compare them to other products. If this is the case, then your marketing has failed. Branded products show their prices, as do no-name brands. We don't need to be told that the branded product is better (if it even is) because their marketing has already told us that. If you need to explain that your product is better, then I think it's safe to say that your marketing is not working properly.

There is one last thing I will say about this. Don't try and trick people into buying by showing lower prices or hiding prices. For example, have you ever been to a website where they show low prices but by the time you've finished the checkout they've added service fees, P&P, card payment fees, interest, and other hidden costs? I don't know about you, but that makes me not want to buy there again. I'd rather see a higher figure (stating what it includes) than arrive at that higher figure at the end of the checkout. Will deceiving people make you the odd sale that you wouldn't have gotten otherwise? I won't lie, it probably will. The problem is that you will lack when it comes to return clients. You would have lost people's trust, and the chances of you receiving referrals will be very low. In my view, open, honest, and reliable will win the race in the long run.

Take home points:

1. Be as transparent as possible with pricing
2. Give guidelines if you want people to request a quote
3. Try and weed out obvious 'tire kickers' as soon as you can
4. Let your marketing justify your higher prices, if need be
5. Don't hide prices or try and trick people into buying by showing lower prices

This is a popular topic for discussion, and I have done both. Initially I registered but then de-registered after a while. I may be forced to register again, at some point, but not at the time of writing this book. Initially I registered because of some advice I received. The advice was not wrong, just not right for me. I was told that businesses who are registered for VAT will almost expect VAT to be charged. It makes you look more serious as a business, and businesses who are VAT registered won't mind because they can claim it back. It also means that if you go over the threshold, there is no mad panic to register. All of this made sense to me, but I didn't consider one thing. Who were my clients? I have clients ranging from one-man bands to multi-national corporations. The larger businesses didn't care whether I was VAT registered or not (I asked them). Many of the smaller businesses were not VAT registered, so they had to take the VAT hit, which often made me too expensive for them.

I also realised that I wasn't buying stock, so my expenses were low. This meant that I couldn't claim back much VAT. I tried the flat rate scheme, but that was so stacked against me, that I didn't get much back. I eventually calculated that I was losing more in jobs (either the quotes were rejected, or I was having to drop my prices to account for the VAT) than I was claiming back in VAT. I de-registered and have never looked back. This is my story; yours may not be the same. You need to consider to whom you are selling, what you are purchasing and for which you can claim back the VAT, how much you could lose out on by being VAT registered, and how close you may get to the threshold. If you're continually going to get close to the threshold I'd advise registering, or keeping a very close eye on that. The other thing to consider is: what are you trying to portray to others? If you are open with your clients, and tell them that you're a small operation, you may not need to charge VAT. Remember that even large businesses who pay VAT still don't save any money by you being VAT registered. They still pay the VAT, but claim it back. It's no different to you not being VAT registered. These options could change at any time, so it's best to discuss this with your accountant.

Take home points:

1. Consider what you're selling, who you're selling to, and how close you'll get to the threshold
2. Do some maths and see what you stand to gain by charging or not charging VAT
3. If you're already trading, have a word with your big clients and ask them what they think
4. Consider flat rate schemes, if available, but don't assume they will be better
5. Speak to your accountant, as the thresholds and rules can change

Renewal Reminders

Running a business is hard work, and there are a hundred things on your mind constantly, so you don't need to put added pressure on yourself. Another thing about running a business is that there are so many things to do each year; re-occurring things. There are annual legal requirements, contract renewals, insurance renewals, certificate renewals, tax payments, and all sorts of other things that will completely slip your mind if you don't have reminders. My suggestion is to make reminders for yourself for all these things. I've made spreadsheets to do this in the past but, even then, people often miss them because they don't open the spreadsheet. I now have these listed in the spreadsheet, and then set reminders on my calendar to remind me of important dates that I can't forget. When your renewals involve paying someone money, they usually remind you, but governments aren't usually that helpful. Keep a list of all your renewals, set reminders for important dates, and check regularly. Even if you do get notifications, I still like the list because it tells me what I was paying before and what needs to be renewed, so immediately I am aware if the price jumps up. Trust me, missing an important date can leave you in heaps of trouble, and it's simple to keep on top of this with a little discipline.

Take home points:

1. Make a list of all renewals
2. Keep all the key information (policy numbers, costs, etc.)
3. Make diary notes for the important reminders
4. Be disciplined in updating information and checking for upcoming reminders
5. It's a simple task, but getting it wrong can be hugely problematic

Much of this has been included in many other chapters, but I just want to let you know of a few mistakes which I have made, and some others that I see being made over and over again. If you're wondering how to sell your products or services, I would say that other chapters such as Marketing, Advertising, Search Engine Optimisation (SEO), Networking, and others, may be more useful than trying to sell. Desperately trying to sell, usually ends up in desperate measures such as spamming, pushy sales tactics and scripted cold calls. I can tell you that these will only frustrate you and lead to disappointment. You need to build a brand, market properly to your target audience, advertise effectively, and engage on social media. This will bring the business to you, so that you don't have to go chasing it. Make sure that your website is effective (see the Website chapter) and get the SEO up to scratch. All of these things create a whole package which is a good environment for people to buy. If you do this well, you shouldn't have to try and convince or persuade people to buy. You may need to call some people, you may need to send a few messages and emails, but just keep one thing in mind: how does it reflect on your brand?

When I started out I was inexperienced, so I got a list of a hundred local businesses and sent them all a cold email. I just dumped a whole sales message into their inbox and hoped for the best. I got one positive reply, which led to a job. I got about twenty very negative replies, as well as getting my email blacklisted. The one job wasn't worth the blacklisted email, but what about the other ninety-nine people? What did they think of my business? I guess, not highly. I had pretty much upset ninety-nine people to get one sale. Ninety-nine people who could well have bought from me if I did it right. I then scrapped that idea and have never sent a cold email again. People may argue that I just didn't do it right, but I see loads of people complaining about cold sales messages on social media. People buy from people, not cold pushy sales messages. I maintain that you should build your brand, advertise effectively, and engage with people. That will bring the sales to you, which is much less stressful and less damaging than chasing them.

Take home points:

1. Advertising, marketing, brand development, and other aspects can be better than selling
2. Cold calls and emails can often damage your brand, if not done correctly
3. Build relationships with your potential clients; people buy from people
4. Make sure you don't break the law, when contacting people, under data protection rules
5. If you do cold call or email people, consider the effect on your brand if you upset them

SEO

SEO is always changing and a massive area to cover, so I will give you some overviews here. If you really want to get it done properly, I suggest consulting a professional. If you just want to understand what this is, I'll try and explain it. SEO stands for Search Engine Optimisation. This means that your website is created in such a way that search engines can understand it, and therefore show your website when people search for content. This can be quite an involved project, so I can't cover anywhere near all of it here, but I can get you started. Here are some things to do from the start.

Set up all images on your website properly. By this, I mean giving them all an 'alternative text' (the text that shows up what the image is, if it doesn't load properly). This text explains to search engines what your image is. This is very effective in helping search engines to effectively rank your website. Use the key words which you want people to use in their searches. For example, if you're a plumber in South East London, think about what key words people will use to find you. Then, use those key words in your website. Don't overdo it, just make sure you use the right key words. Write some blog posts - those are great to use keywords and also to give your potential clients some more information. Use videos in your website (see the Videos, Blogs, & Podcasts and Website chapters). Make sure you label and tag them correctly, so that the search engines know what they are about. In the early days of websites there were tricks that you could do to get ahead, but as we progress those are rapidly depleting. It is fast becoming a simple solution. If your website is good for humans, it should be good for SEO. The search engine demands are getting more and more 'human', so just make your website good for visitors and make sure everything is labelled correctly.

That will get you off to a good head start. If you want to delve deeper into this when you have some funds, go ahead, it can be a great source of leads. At least get the basics right when you start, to give yourself the best chance possible. Lastly, take advantages of any favouritism shown by search engines. Say, for example, a major search engine owns a website where you can publish your videos. It would make sense to use that video publishing website for your videos, and then embed them into your website, if you want to rank highly in that search engine.

Take home points:

1. Label all images and complete the 'alternative text'
2. Use videos and make sure they're tagged properly
3. Make your website good for human visitors
4. Use specific key words in your website and blog posts

5. Take advantage of any favouritism shown by search engines

Slow Patches

Depending on what industry you're in, enquiries could be like waiting for a bus - none come for ages and then three come at once. It can be very much up and down. It does improve, but you will always have slow patches and busy patches. This is about what to do during the slow patches. I have some suggestions that I have done myself, over the years. Firstly: get ahead. Think of all the time-consuming exercises like creating marketing content, brochures, new products or services, website content, social media posts, videos, adverts, blog posts, and email newsletters. Can any of them be done before they are required? Absolutely. I would make a note of all these things that needed to be done then, as soon as I had a quiet patch, I'd get stuck into these.

The other thing I would do is have a fall-back project. My fall-back project was this book so, if you're reading this, it was time well spent. I saw this as a potential source of extra income, but I didn't want to set aside hours when I could be earning money. I was already well ahead with my marketing and advertising materials, my website was up to date, as were all the brochures and products, so I decided to write a book. Every hour, day, or even longer, when I didn't have work to do, I'd write. This not only allowed me to write this book, but it also kept me busy. I saw it as important to keep busy because my mind is powerful and I wanted to be using it in a positive way. When I was writing, my mind would be creative and positive. In fact, I often got upset when I was in the swing of things and work would come in, but that's a small price to pay. If I spent that time waiting for work I never would have written this book, but I think I also would have worried myself into a state. I would much rather be productive than worry. The other good side about doing these things when you have time is because then you don't have to do them when you don't have time. I plan social media marketing content up to a year in advance. When I am busy it takes me seconds to post what I planned, rather than much longer, to create content when I need it. Another thing I do is to have a list of tasks which need to be done at some stage. You know the ones - things that are not urgent, but would be good to do at some stage. I dive into a list of them when I have nothing to do. Again, it keeps me busy and I keep productive.

When you're busy you'll be surprised how many tasks become urgent, that you could have done already when you were looking for things to do. Make sure you take that time to get ahead and try not to worry. When the work comes in you can get stuck in and don't have to worry about the other tasks, as they are already done. Lastly, if there are any known slow patches, try and arrange annual leave for then, if possible. I know that no one ever calls me between Christmas and New Year, so I always take that time off. This means that I am working when people could get in touch, and I'm off when people are not likely to contact me. I then don't stress, and can relax, because I planned for that down time.

Take home points:

1. Look ahead for tasks which can be done now, that will help you later, and make a note of them
2. Have a 'fall-back' task at the ready, so you can do that if all else fails
3. Make a note of all the nice-to-do-if-you-have-the-time tasks to get done
4. Don't worry about work; keep yourself busy and trust in your process
5. Try and plan annual leave around known slow patches

Social Media

I was considering writing about each social media platform, and explaining how best to tackle each one, but then I realised two things. I don't use many of them so I have no idea how to tackle them and, by the time you read this, we may have loads more. Social media has its faults, and it can be extremely dangerous, but it is a marketing and advertising gold-mine and the platforms know that. More and more platforms try to push you into paying to get eyes on your content, but there are still ways to share content for free. Whether you pay or go the free route, there are things to consider. The first thing I will say is that you don't have to be on all social media channels. When I started out I looked at large businesses and they seemed to have social media accounts on all channels, so I followed suit. The problem was that I didn't have teams of staff managing these accounts, I was doing it myself. Let me tell you - social media can eat up all your time, if you're not careful. Trying to run accounts on all platforms, being relevant on each, and interacting properly can be a full-time job. So, what should you do then?

Here's my advice. Look at the brand you are creating and decide who is your ideal client (see Creating a Brand and Target Audience). Where does your ideal client hang out and which platform best suits your brand? With a little luck, those two may well be the same platform. Also, which platform do you enjoy? If you hate using a platform, but your clients are there and it suits your brand, it may be an idea to outsource. Either that, or you just need to get on and do it. I found that I wouldn't engage as much on platforms that I didn't like, and that didn't help me at all. I was on four social media platforms to start with. I then realised that one of them was complete vanity metrics and brought in absolutely no business, as the views and comments on that platform were made by people who never were going to be clients. I stopped that. I then realised that another platform was not bringing in any business, and it was a platform that I hated to be on so I never interacted. I stopped that too. I was then left with the last two, one of which I didn't really participate but had a presence just because people were following me (I'm not sure why). The last platform was the one I enjoyed the most, it was where all my potential clients hung out, and it was best suited to my brand. Absolute win. At the time of writing this book, over 60% of all my new business is coming directly or indirectly from this channel. It also means that all the time I was spending on four channels can now be used to make really good use of one channel. If not, it could be used for other things too, but the point is that I'm not wasting time on sites that will never generate me any return on investment. Remember to include your time when calculating ROI. How did I figure this out?

Analysis. If you've read this book from the start you'll know by now that I analyse pretty much everything, and this was no exception. I knew which campaigns worked best on what platforms and I learned how to advertise effectively on at least one of them (the one that worked). This enabled me to pick the right platform for me, and I knew the best tactic to deploy on that site, which led to great return on investment. That's the final point in this chapter: play the game. Each social media site expects something different and they each have a way to do things. You need to figure that out to really thrive. I'm not suggesting that you do what everyone else is doing, but there are certain ways to get traction on each platform; things that are acceptable and things that aren't. If you play the game right, you're on the platform that you and your ideal client enjoy, you're interacting and you're on point with your marketing, you'll see the results.

Take home points:

1. You don't need to be on all social media channels
2. Ask what channel(s) best fits your brand, and where your ideal clients hang out
3. Hopefully you'll pick a channel that you enjoy, because you need to engage
4. Play the game that the platform demands to see success
5. Analyse the data so that you know what works and if you have a good ROI

Spreadsheets

If you've read just about any of the other chapters you'll realise that this chapter was inevitable, and probably the only one that I can write with any kind of authority. I use spreadsheets for just about anything, and have done so for many years. Long before I started Spreadsheet Solutions I was using spreadsheets for business. Why? Because Excel was readily available, and I found it easy to make what I wanted. A professionally made purpose-built spreadsheet will almost always be cheaper than custom software, because it is quicker to produce. This means that even if you get a spreadsheet made by someone like me, you'll still save money. Spreadsheets are tremendously useful and can be used for all aspects of your business. In fact, many of the chapters of this book mention spreadsheets, and many of these chapters made their way into this book because I use spreadsheets for them. Reminders, warnings, financial records, data analysis, reporting, dashboards, process tracking, project management, HR, sales, marketing, etc. The list goes on and I've made spreadsheets to help with them all.

If you don't use spreadsheets for your business, I would suggest that you explore the option at least. If you can make them yourself, then go for it. If you're not sure, or you'd rather get them done properly, please get hold of me. I won't say too much about spreadsheets here, but I will say this: make sure they're made properly, and put various checks in place, to ensure that the calculations are correct. You begin to rely on them and take them as correct. If they're not, that can cause problems. If you're in any doubt, it may be best to get them made by a professional.

Take home points:

1. Consider using spreadsheets for your business
2. They are not just for financial records, but for most aspects of business
3. They are very cost effective, compared to custom programmed software
4. They are easy to make but, if you're not sure, get a professional involved
5. They could provide solutions you didn't think were possible

Running your own business can be a very lonely place, especially when you don't employ anyone. Also, your friends and family won't be of much support if they don't also run a business. Yes, they can possibly help you practically or financially, but they won't understand what it is like. Only other business owners know. My advice is to find a core group of business owners that you trust, to get a network of people to turn to if need be. There are paid groups, but I simply asked around and a few of us started a mastermind group where we could chat through issues, pose questions, and get advice. I found this very helpful. Sometimes you don't have massive issues to deal with, you just need to run an idea past some people. I found that family and friends often were too supportive and would just agree with you. I needed someone to challenge me and offer other, possibly better, ideas. I also needed to talk to someone who knew what I was experiencing and had relevant advice. This group helped with that. You have social media and networking events where you could turn to someone for advice, but having a closed group of people can help if the problem is slightly bigger or more personal. It helps to have some people who won't judge you, but try to help when you need it. There are always problems which need professional help so, if you need that, please seek it. I'm not suggesting that these groups will fulfil such a need, but they do fill the gap between professional help and social media connections.

I need to say something else about your wellbeing and support, but you may not like it. Running a business is not for everyone and it is hard work, especially at the start. There may well be months when you don't know where the money will come from, and you're already on the 20th of the month. It is stressful. People earning salaries don't know this stress. It requires tremendous faith and resilience, and I've seen it break strong people. I'm not saying this to put you off, I'm saying it so that you are prepared. If starting a business is your way of working less, or simply not having to answer to a boss, I would suggest that you reconsider. I would advise that you only go down this route if you are sure, and if you're willing to stick it out. Then make sure you have people available, so you can support one other, because you (and they) will need it. If you do find that it's all too much, and a paid salary starts to sound irresistible, there is no shame in returning to regular/conventional employment. Yes, I believe that there are advantages to determination and not giving up, but not when it leads to you being broken. There's a time to fight and not give up, and there's a time to realise when you're on the wrong path and pick another one. My advice is to get yourself a group of other business owners, for you to support and also be supported by, and not be too proud to seek more help if needed.

Take home points:

1. Running a business is hard work and not for everyone
2. Family and friends may not understand what it's like to run a business
3. Get into a group of business owners where you can support each other
4. Get more professional help if needed, don't try to be a hero
5. There is no shame in going back to conventional employment if the business doesn't work

I've mentioned this in many of the other chapters. Marketing, advertising, social media activity, networking, brand creation, and even your internal processes can come down to one thing. Who is your ideal client? Many people answer this question simply by saying that it is everyone. This is often not the case but, even if it is true, still ask yourself this question. That way you have someone to whom you can market, and someone to keep in mind when considering all the other relevant aspects of your business. Some business owners target a certain audience even when they don't need to. Let's say that you sold insurance. You could sell to anyone but just saying that you sell insurance doesn't particularly appeal to anyone. What if you said that you sold life insurance to dads? Then you could market your life insurance to men and, particularly, fathers. You could have adverts showing dads how important life insurance is for their families. Now suddenly you're appealing to me, as a man and a father, and you're more likely to get my attention.

Niching can be a powerful tool and can help immensely with your marketing and branding. Even if you don't niche, it's still a good idea to earmark a particular client. You then have a target to aim for. You then also have people in mind, when creating marketing material, so you know that it will meet an emotional need of the client. This doesn't mean that you can't help others, it just gives you the focus that you need. In the above example: if a mum contacted the person for insurance, they would still help her, but they just don't market to her specifically. When I started out, I was too scared to do this. I thought that it would lessen the pool of potential clients, and therefore lessen the income. I wanted as wide a net as possible to catch the most fish. Here's the problem: if the net is too wide, you may not catch anything. I've referenced accountants quite often in this book, so let's look at them. Let's say you were an accountant and you said that you could help any business owner (which you probably can). You then tell me about how reliable you are and that you will save me money, blah blah blah. I've heard it all before. Yes, you're honest, affordable, and reliable, but so is everyone else (according to them). Why should I use you? Your marketing is aimed at everyone, but there are so many accountants around; why should I pick you? Here's something to consider: who would you rather work with? Do you have more experience in any industry? If you said that you were an accountant for builders, what then?

Theoretically you are drastically decreasing the size of your pool of clients, but you have a much bigger chance of catching a fish in a small pond. You can now target all your advertising to builders. You can create your brand around them, post content relevant to them, and connect with them on social media and at networking events. You can also make it clear to others when they should recommend you. If I know you, I may not recommend you as an accountant because I know twenty others. However, you may be the only accountant I know who specifically work with builders. So, if I get asked by a builder, I will recommend you. See how it works? You either can have a little chance of catching many fish, or a larger chance of catching fewer fish. Which option is better? It depends on what you're selling, who's buying, how good your marketing is, and how many others do what you do. I couldn't niche regarding my target audience, but the services I supplied (making spreadsheets) was quite niche. Anyone asked for a spreadsheet to be made, and my name was thrown around. You need to get yourself known for something then, when that need arises, you'll be remembered or referred. This requires quite a bit of thought before deciding, so make some notes and consider your ideal client. Maybe ask for some feedback from others. This decision will affect many other aspects of your business, so it's worth some time to consider.

Take home points:

1. Think about who is your ideal client
2. Consider niching if you are competing with others for the same clients
3. Get known for something specific, so that you will be remembered
4. Niching or targeting specific people will help with many aspects of business

5. Target marketing won't necessarily stop other business from happening

I constantly see questions about these - people wondering which they should do, and why. Again, this comes down to your target market, marketing, and branding, but there are some things to consider. Firstly, blog posts are good for your SEO (see the chapter on that), so I would advise doing blog posts from the start. Also, you don't need to do them regularly (unless you've promised your readers), so you simply can add these as inspiration strikes. They're also a great way to show people how you can help and to get people to your website. When I share a blog post on social media, I usually get a few people looking around the website after they have read the post. The only downside to blog posts is if your posts are damaging your brand. If you struggle to write blogs, or if you're not sure how your views come across, ask some people to read what you've done and get some feedback. I would say that blogs should be one of the first things you do once your website is up and running, as they are relatively easy and good to share on social media.

As for videos, let's break them up into two categories. Firstly, advert or explainer videos are great, especially if you offer a product or service with which people are not familiar. I would also suggest having at least one video on your website home page. At the time of writing this book, that was one thing which would score you some major points with the big search engines. Not only that, but a potential client can watch a thirty second video and, if done correctly, they will get more out of that than trying to figure out what you offer. You do need to consider all the aspects of your brand, marketing strategy, target audience, etc., when making these videos, but they are very useful to have. Not only to embed on your website, but also to post on social media.

The other kind of video content, which I will put into the same category as podcasts, is a regular video series. This is also very useful, but more demanding. I did a video series of twelve videos before writing this book, and am considering more, but it was very time consuming. I did videos where I interviewed some other business owners, and thoroughly enjoyed it, but it was hard work getting twelve people lined up and finding the time to record all the episodes. Then still editing and creating web pages for each, then planning social media content to promote them. I also needed to upload all the videos and make sure I had the correct links for social media. It was a lot of hard work. Having said that, once set up, it did run itself for three months, providing me with useful content. My point is that if you take on a regular video series or podcast, make sure you know what you're in for before you start. Plan and see what's required, before committing. I see so many of these initiatives start and then five episodes in they get fed up and stop. I would advise having done a few before you launch them, so you're already ahead (unless you're doing them live, which involves even more thought).

The bottom line is this: get stuck into some blog posts and make some videos to explain why people should buy from you. If you want to do a video series or podcast, make sure that it is relevant to your target market, and make sure that you're in it for the long haul. I'd also suggest making the whole process as simple as possible. For example, it's exciting making the first video so you throw in all the bells and whistles while editing. By the 10th one you wish you had kept it simple. Keep it simple from the start, so that it is sustainable and the quality doesn't drop.

Take home points:

1. Blogs are a good way to start building content and helping your SEO
2. Videos showing why people should buy from you are a good idea
3. If you want to do a video series or podcast, make sure you're set for the long haul
4. Keep all your content in line with your branding and marketing strategies
5. Try and keep a theme throughout your content, and keep the process as simple as possible

Websites

I knew nothing about websites when I started my business, other than the fact that I needed one. I have learnt so much, but I won't bore you with the technical stuff. There are a few things that you need to know before deciding what to do. I won't mention specific names, as they may change or I may upset some people, but the principle is important. Think of a website as a car, and a host as a garage. You need a car and a garage to store it, simple as that. Now think of different platforms (where you can create a website or get one created for you) as a make of car. As with makes of cars, some are better than others, some are good for specific purposes, and some are just troublesome from start to finish. It's the same with platforms. Some are more difficult to work with, so DIY business owners often ignore them. Others seem easier at first but then, after a few years, they don't do what you need them to when you grow and advance. The worst aspect (in my opinion) is that some offer the car and garage in one. They market it as a good thing, but, think about it. You are now stuck with that car and that garage, and you can't leave.

I made sure that I used the platform that was the most versatile (as I grew and needed more) and that I was not tied down to one host. This means that I can take my website and change hosts very easily if I wish. Yes, it was slightly harder at first because it was not the easiest platform to learn, but now that I know how to do it, I have endless possibilities. The platform I use is the most widely used platform as I write this; there are very little restrictions on what is possible with it (even if I personally can't do it, someone can). I can also decide where I host it, so I can make sure that the host is local, cost effective and on the ball. That is important to me, because it is horrible when your website is down, and potential clients can't get in touch, especially if you're selling products directly from your website. I'm not suggesting that you do exactly what I've done, maybe you don't need to. I'm just saying that you should know what you're getting into from the start. I hear of so many people starting out with what seems easiest at the time and regretting it a year or two later. I've seen people re-create entire websites because they couldn't move their website and they reached the limit of what the platform could do. If you're not sure about this, ask someone that you trust. Just be aware that many businesses try to dazzle you with tech-speak when this is involved. If you don't understand, and they won't explain so that you understand, walk away. You don't need to know all the ins and outs, but you should understand the limitations of the platform, where it is hosted, and how flexible it is if you wish to change or move the website.

The last thing about this is the domain name - the name which you type into the browser to visit your website. Make sure you own that domain. Many web creators have an all-in-one offer, and they own your domain. Firstly, that gives them serious potential to hold you to ransom later but, secondly, it also leaves you out of the loop should they disappear. Make sure you own the domain, make sure you have administrator rights to it, and make sure you can choose where it is hosted and that you can move it, if required. Anything less than this and I would suggest that you may find yourself in trouble.

That's the technical part, then there is also the creative part. My first website had so much information on it that it scared most visitors. I'm very much a collect-as-much-information-as-I-can kind of buyer, so I assumed everyone was. Your website needs to be a simple process to take a potential client from someone looking around to someone buying. Yes, you can have other things on your website, but the journey from the home page to them buying should be as short as possible. I got this wrong for many years. I now have all the extra content behind some buttons if people deliberately want to find it. Most people go from the home page to where they can purchase as quickly as possible. You also need to make sure that your website layout and design encourage this, as well as work with your brand image and tie in with your marketing content. Clients should flow from your point of contact, to your website, and into the sales process. This can be very hard to achieve, but that is the goal. One thing I did was to look at my website as if I was a potential client. What was my reaction to it? As soon as I saw the old website, I decided I wouldn't shop there. That was a massive incentive to change, and I am much happier now than I was then!

Take home points:

1. Make sure you own your domain and have administrator rights to your website
2. Make sure that you can host your website where you want
3. Get your website as clear and simple as possible to get people to buy
4. View your website as if you were a potential client and see how you would react
5. Have your website layout and design in keeping with your brand

If you manage to crack this, let me know. There are so many books, blog posts, and courses based on this, so I won't say too much. I will say that starting and running a business is time consuming. If you're running the business from home (see the relevant chapter) then the lines between work and rest can be blurred. Also, I find that I never really switch off. I could do it when I was employed, but I struggle now. You get a good marketing idea in the shower, and spend the next hour thinking about it. Next thing you know you're back in work mode again and you were supposed to be relaxing. Then you throw in a husband/wife/partner and possibly children, and you realise that you have no free time. It's tough. I haven't mastered this yet, and my wife may well read this back to me at some stage, but you need to try and find time for all these things. Prioritise what is important at the time, and then leave the rest or outsource it.

You may work mornings, you may work evenings, you may work flat out during the week and never on weekends. You may work for eleven months so you can take one month off; there are no rules. That is one of the pros of having your own business, just don't neglect anything or anyone. Spending time with loved ones is essential, especially children (see the Working & Children chapter) and spouses/partners (see the Working with a Partner chapter). If you can do so, I would advise that you have a room for work, like an office. Then you can close that door when it is family time and put work on hold until you next need to work. I know this often is not possible, but at least try and set some time to do different things. I can tell you that if you don't, then managing a business could run away with your time, attention, and eventually your life. Sometimes you need to be dedicated and disciplined at the expense of other areas of your life, but that should only be temporary. If you find this is becoming a trend, assess it and make some changes. I know this is hard to do, because you feel the pressure, but you need to. The sooner you get into this habit the better. This is also why I encourage people to get their processes as efficient as possible. The less you need to do to make the most profit, the better. That will then leave you with more time to enjoy, and more resources to use to enjoy it. I often used to find myself working for the sake of it - it's 2pm, and 2pm is work time, so I must work. I would then be doing work that wasn't important and usually wasn't necessary. I'd then have inspiration strike at 5pm, I'd continue until 9pm and then I was exhausted. I rather should have stopped at 2pm and watched a movie. Then I would have had some down time and still had an inspired work session later. You can be flexible, you just need to recognise all the aspects of your life and make sure you set some time aside for each, whenever that may be.

Take home points:

1. Find a routine that gives you time for all aspects of life
2. Put work first if you need to, but only for a limited period
3. Be as efficient as you can, so that you're not wasting time
4. Recognise when you're working for the sake of it, and change
5. You don't need to stick to office hours, just make time to relax

Most new business owners will need to do this for some time, at least at the start, and there are various things to consider. Firstly, can you set aside a room which is just your office? If you can, I would suggest doing this. It is so much easier to have work space and home space, so that they don't get mixed, especially if you have children. The office is for work, the rest of the house is for family. I found that working from home was more difficult than I thought, not because I wasn't motivated, but because I did so with a young son. He didn't care if daddy was working when he wanted my attention. I found that some simple planning helped me.

Firstly, I knew when I was at my best and when I wasn't. I'm not a morning person, so anything done before 9am needs to be checked. However, I seem to hit my stride in the afternoon and tend to want to work after 5pm when I am in full flow. I took all of this into account and made the necessary adjustments. I worked while my son was at pre-school, then took a break for lunch and the short period after lunch when my wife worked (she also works with me from home - see the chapter about working with a partner). My son then went down for a nap in the afternoon when I did more work, then my wife took over after that and took my son for a walk so I could get more work done. We then had some family time in the evening, and put our son to bed slightly later, so he only woke up at 8am which was in time to get him ready for pre-school. Now that routine may be completely wrong for you, but the thought process should be the same. When do you work best, when do you need to be available for other people (such as children), and when do you need to be working (for clients)? Often there is work that needs to be done at certain times, but usually there is a lot of work that can be done when it is convenient to you. You need to find a routine that works for you.

Now I'm going to tell you something else, but I feel like a hypocrite because I have not yet mastered this. It is a current action which I am trying to change, so I thought I'd mention it to you. You don't have to be working for the sake of it, and you don't have to feel guilty if you don't work eight hours a day. Often I will sit looking for things to do, because it is now 'time' to work. I then realise how unproductive I can be at times. I then feel guilty because I was unproductive. I am not lazy, and I possibly tend to work harder than I should, so why do I feel like this? I don't know, but I do know that it is not helpful. I'm always up to date with client work, I'm always ahead with marketing, I always have a side project on the go (like this book), so why beat myself up when I don't have anything to do for an hour? Fortunately, this book isn't about my emotional issues, so I'll just let you know that you don't need to feel this way. If you're not feeling it, and there is nothing pressing, take an hour off and watch some TV or go for a walk. You work hard enough, you deserve it (and yes, I'm talking to me, too).

I also find that on occasions when I have just taken an hour off because I wasn't feeling like working, I have come back even stronger and been much more productive afterwards. That is something to consider. I have also taken some slightly more dramatic actions in the past when I've had important projects to finish. I've left the child with my wife and gone down to a coffee shop to work. Yes, it's a noisy public place, but at least I don't have someone tugging on my sleeve the whole time, calling "Daddy". Having said this, you do need to make sure you set aside time for your family, so please also see the chapter entitled Work / Life Balance. I'm not going to lie, it is hard to get this right, and you may make mistakes. Go easy on yourself and try to find what works for you. It may seem crazy to other people, but if it works for you, go with it.

Take home points:

1. Try and set your office aside in your house, if possible
2. Find a routine that works for you, around your responsibilities and family
3. Use the times when you're 'in the zone' to do quality work
4. Don't feel guilty for not working all the time

5. Get out the house for a change of scenery, when required

Working with a Partner

This was initially going to be about working with your significant other, but now it is about that and working with a business partner. Let's look at the significant other first. I set up a business with my wife, and we work together. Up until the time of writing this book we were working in separate rooms, due to space, but we're now planning a move and plan to work in the same room in the future. Some couples may say that this is a stupid idea, and maybe it is for them, but not for us. We like working with each other. This is very much something to be considered, though. You do end up seeing your partner all the time. Wake up, work, lunch, work, dinner, family time, bedtime, weekends, always together. If you can handle this, then I think it's a good idea. If you can't, then please don't work together. We chose this for the flexibility and support. We live in the UK but most of our family are overseas, so we don't have the support which most other parents do have. We chose to be self-sufficient and work from home. We knew what we were getting ourselves into and chose it. This is not for everyone, though. If you enjoy your space and time at work, and don't want to be in each other's faces twenty-four hours a day, then I'd consider not working together. It also depends on what work you both do, and if it is even viable. My wife and I both decided what we wanted to do, and they were compatible, so they went together well.

The downside of doing everything together is that there are some dull patches when we go out together (on the rare occasion). We end up talking about work, our child, and the home. When you don't do anything without the other person, they know everything that is going on. It makes for quite boring conversations, but that may not be a big deal to you. Let's now look at working with a business partner. Please see the chapter entitled Collaborations because much of that applies here too. Do you share the same values? Do you have the same goals and ambitions? Are you both contributing? Are your roles defined and is there an overlap of responsibilities? Many people start business partnerships with friends because "What could possibly go wrong?" and then end up losing a friend and business partner. Running a business is stressful, and conflicting views and agendas can add more stress to the picture. Please think through carefully before engaging in a partnership. Yes, many have done it, and it may well benefit you both in the long run, but it does come with challenges. Think about the pros and cons and why you need to do it. Think about what could happen if it went wrong, and if you could deal with that. If you can do it on your own I would suggest that, but ultimately it is up to you. Just go in with your eyes open and be clear what is expected from the start.

Take home points:

1. Consider your relationship with your significant other, before working together
2. Consider mutual values, agendas, and plans when working with any partner
3. Go in with your eyes open and make sure you have a clear plan
4. Try and keep business roles and responsibilities defined and separate
5. If you're in any doubt, my advice would be to go it alone

Conclusion

Well, there you have it. Forty chapters about forty aspects of running a business. I hope you have enjoyed it and found some useful information. Some of what I have written may not apply to you, and some of my advice may not be relevant, but I hope that this at least has given you food for thought. If this helps you not to make some of the mistakes that I did, then it was worth it. None of these chapters were designed to give you all the answers, as there are probably entire books written on each of them, and I couldn't possibly go into detail on each. I just wanted to give you an overview on each ,and help you to know what to look out for and consider.

Remember that this is your business, and you are responsible. You don't have to make it like anyone else's business, and you don't have to follow any advice. I hope that you will take from this book what is relevant to you, and use it to make the right decisions for your business, and I hope that you see success faster than I did. Go into all decisions with your eyes open, and be as informed as you can. I wish you all the success.

Printed in Poland
by Amazon Fulfillment
Poland Sp. z o.o., Wrocław

64130480R00067